# MAUI TRAVEL GUIDE 2024

## A Guide To Exploring Maui's Wonders, Culture, and Adventures.

### BY

## Marcos A. Hurd

# Table Of Contents

4

# Chapter 1. Introduction to Maui

*Explore the beauty of Maui, also known as the Valley Isle paradise, with its picturesque beaches, verdant scenery, and rich cultural experiences that await you on this captivating Hawaiian island.*

## Overview of Maui

Maui, often referred to as the "Valley Isle," is the second-largest island in the Hawaiian archipelago and is renowned for its stunning natural beauty, diverse landscapes, and rich cultural heritage. Located in the Central Pacific, Maui attracts millions of visitors each year seeking adventure, relaxation, and a taste of authentic Hawaiian culture.

The island is characterized by its contrasting geography, with lush rainforests, cascading waterfalls, volcanic landscapes, and pristine beaches. At the heart of Maui lies the towering Haleakalā volcano, a dormant shield volcano that forms more than 75% of the island's landmass. Rising 10,023 feet above sea level, Haleakalā National Park is a haven for outdoor enthusiasts, offering opportunities for hiking, camping, and stargazing amidst otherworldly terrain.

Maui's coastline is equally captivating, boasting some of the world's most renowned beaches. The west coast is home to the resort areas of Kaanapali and Kapalua, where visitors can indulge in luxury accommodations, championship golf courses, and upscale shopping and dining. Meanwhile, the south coast features the picturesque towns of Wailea and Makena, known for their pristine white sands and crystal-clear waters, perfect for snorkeling, scuba diving, and whale watching during the winter months.

Away from the coast, Maui's interior is a paradise for nature lovers and adventure seekers. The scenic road to Hana, famously known as the Hana Highway, winds through lush rainforests, past dramatic sea cliffs, and over countless waterfalls. Along the journey, travelers can explore bamboo forests, swim in freshwater pools, and visit cultural landmarks such as the Seven Sacred Pools at Ohe'o Gulch.

Maui's cultural heritage is deeply rooted in its Polynesian past, and visitors have the opportunity to immerse themselves in traditional Hawaiian customs and practices. The island is home to numerous historical sites and cultural attractions, including the Maui Arts and Cultural Center, which showcases local artists and performers, and the 'Iao Valley State Park, a sacred site steeped in Hawaiian mythology and history.

The spirit of aloha permeates every aspect of life on Maui, from its vibrant festivals and events to its warm and welcoming residents. Visitors are encouraged to participate in traditional ceremonies, such as the Hawaiian luau, where they can feast on local cuisine, watch captivating hula performances, and learn about the island's cultural heritage.

Maui's culinary scene is a reflection of its diverse cultural influences, blending traditional Hawaiian ingredients with flavors from around the world. From roadside food trucks serving fresh poke bowls to upscale restaurants offering farm-to-table cuisine, the island caters to every palate and preference.

In addition to its natural beauty and cultural attractions, Maui offers a wide range of recreational activities for visitors of all ages. Whether it's surfing on the legendary waves of Ho'okipa Beach, zip-lining through the lush valleys of Upcountry Maui, or embarking on a sunset cruise along the scenic coastline, there's no shortage of adventures to be had on the Valley Isle.

As one of the most sought-after destinations in the world, Maui continues to captivate the hearts of travelers with its unparalleled beauty, warm hospitality, and timeless allure. Whether you're looking for relaxation, adventure, or a deeper connection with nature and culture, Maui offers unforgettable experiences that will keep you coming back for more.

## Brief History and Culture

Maui's history and culture are deeply intertwined with its natural environment and the Polynesian people who settled the island over a millennium ago.

The earliest inhabitants of Maui were Polynesian voyagers who arrived on double-hulled canoes from other Pacific islands around 1,500 years ago. These settlers brought with them their language, customs, and traditions, which laid the foundation for Maui's unique cultural identity.

In the centuries that followed, Maui was ruled by powerful chieftains who controlled various regions of the island. One of the most renowned rulers was King Pi'ilani, who is credited with constructing extensive irrigation systems and establishing a centralized government. In the late 18th century, Maui, along with the rest of the Hawaiian Islands, was unified under the rule of King Kamehameha I, who established the Hawaiian Kingdom.

The arrival of European explorers and traders in the late 18th century marked a significant turning point in Maui's history. Captain James Cook was one of the first Europeans to encounter the Hawaiian Islands in 1778. Subsequent contact with Westerners brought about profound changes to Hawaiian society, including the introduction of new technologies, diseases, and Western influences.

In the early 19th century, Christian missionaries from New England arrived in Hawaii, including Maui, with the aim of converting the native population to Christianity. While the missionaries played a role in the education and modernization of Hawaiian society, their presence also led to the decline of traditional Hawaiian beliefs and practices.

The mid-19th century saw the rise of the sugar industry on Maui, fueled by the demand for sugar in the global market. Large plantations were established across the island, attracting laborers from Asia, Europe, and other parts of the world. The influx of immigrant workers contributed to the cultural diversity of Maui, with communities of Japanese, Chinese, Portuguese, and Filipino descent leaving lasting imprints on the island's cultural landscape.

In 1898, Hawaii was annexed by the United States, leading to further changes in Maui's social, political, and economic structure. American influence became more pronounced with the establishment of military bases, commercial interests, and tourist infrastructure.

Today Maui is a vibrant multicultural community that embraces modern influences while honoring its rich heritage. The island's economy is based on tourism, agriculture and trade, with special attention paid to preserving its natural beauty and cultural traditions. Maui residents continue to practice and perpetuate traditional customs such as hula, lei making, and celebrating cultural festivals, keeping the spirit of Aloha alive on the Valley Island.

## Religious Practice in Maui

Maui's religious practices are diverse and reflect the island's multicultural population and rich cultural heritage. Some of the major religious traditions practiced on the island include:

### Christianity:
Like other parts of Hawaii, Christianity, especially Protestantism and Catholicism, is widespread on Maui. There are many churches of various denominations throughout the island,

and both islanders and visitors attend religious services.

## Hawaiian Religion:
Traditional Hawaiian religious practices, known as "Hawaiian spirituality," are still revered and revered by many Maui residents. These practices are deeply rooted in the connection between the Hawaiian people and the land, sea, and natural elements. Ceremonies, rituals, and offerings are performed to honor Hawaiian gods and goddesses, such as Pele (goddess of fire and volcanoes) and Lono (god of fertility and agriculture).

## Buddhism:
Buddhism has a strong influence on Maui, especially among the island's Asian immigrant community. Maui is home to several Buddhist temples and meditation centers that offer spiritual guidance, meditation sessions, and cultural events.

## Hinduism:

Hindu traditions are practiced in a small but vibrant community on the island of Maui. The island is home to the Sri Narayani Peedam Temple, located in Makawao City, which serves as the spiritual and cultural center for the island's Hindus.

## New Age and Spiritual Movement:
Maui has long been a magnet for those seeking spiritual enlightenment and alternative lifestyles. The island is famous for its New Age and spiritual movements, attracting people who practice yoga, meditation, holistic healing and other alternative therapies.

## Other Religions:
Maui's religious landscape also includes small communities practicing Islam, Judaism, and a variety of other religious traditions. These communities may be relatively small compared to Christianity or Hawaiian spirituality, but they contribute to the island's religious diversity and cultural heritage.

Maui's religious practices reflect the island's multicultural identity and deep respect for the natural world. Islanders and visitors are encouraged to respect and appreciate the diverse religious traditions that coexist harmoniously on Valley Island.

# What makes Maui a Famous Tourist's Paradise

Maui's status as a famous tourist paradise is attributed to a combination of factors that appeal to travelers from around the world:

## Natural Beauty:

Maui boasts breathtaking natural landscapes, including pristine beaches, lush rainforests, cascading waterfalls, and dramatic volcanic formations. From the iconic Road to Hana to the stunning vistas of Haleakalā National Park, the island offers endless opportunities for exploration and adventure amidst some of the most picturesque scenery on Earth.

## Outdoor Activities:

Maui is a playground for outdoor enthusiasts, offering a wide range of activities such as snorkeling, scuba diving, surfing, windsurfing, kiteboarding, hiking, ziplining, horseback riding, and golfing. With warm tropical waters and year-round sunshine, visitors can enjoy their favorite outdoor activities surrounded by stunning natural beauty.

## Whale watching:

Maui is one of the best places in the world to watch whales. Winter is especially the time when humpback whales migrate to the warm waters of the Hawaiian Islands to breed and give birth. Visitors can see these majestic creatures up close on boat tours or from the shore, creating an unforgettable wildlife experience.

## Cultural Experience:

Maui's rich cultural heritage is evident in traditional Hawaiian customs, arts and festivals. Visitors can immerse themselves in the island's cultural traditions through activities such as attending a luau, learning to play the hula or ukulele, exploring historic sites, and sampling local cuisine.

## Luxury Resorts and Hotels:

Maui has a variety of hotels, from luxury resorts and boutique hotels to vacation rentals and eco-lodges. Many of these hotels are located along Maui's beautiful coastline, offering guests unparalleled ocean views, world-class amenities and first-class service.

## Farm-to-Table Cuisine:

Maui's culinary scene is known for its farm-to-table cuisine, which uses fresh, local ingredients from the island's fertile lands and bountiful waters. Visitors can enjoy a variety of restaurants, from casual beachfront eateries to award-winning restaurants led by celebrity chefs.

## Warm Hospitality:

The Aloha spirit is alive and well on Maui. The people of Maui are known for their warmth, friendliness, and hospitality. Visitors are welcomed with open arms and are made to feel like an ohana (family), creating a welcoming and inclusive atmosphere that enhances the overall travel experience.

## Accessibility:

Maui is easily accessible via direct flights from major cities in the United States and Canada, as well as connecting flights from international destinations. Once on the island, getting around is convenient with well-maintained roads and a variety of transportation options, including rental cars, shuttles, and public buses.

Maui's combination of natural beauty, outdoor activities, cultural experiences, luxury accommodations, warm hospitality, and accessibility makes it a famous tourist paradise that continues to captivate the hearts of travelers from around the globe.

# Chapter 2: Planning Your Trip to Maui

*Make planning your Maui trip a breeze! Discover exciting activities, lodging options, and important pointers for a memorable vacation in this tropical heaven.*

## When to Visit

The best time to visit Maui depends on your preferences and what you want to see during your trip. But generally, the best times to visit Maui are spring (April to May) and fall (September to November). Here's why:

### Weather:

During the spring and fall, Maui experiences pleasant weather with temperatures in the 70s to 80s Fahrenheit (about 24 to 29 degrees Celsius). These months typically feature less rainfall and milder temperatures compared to peak tourist season, making outdoor activities more enjoyable.

## Crowds:
Visiting in the off-season means fewer crowds compared to the peak tourist seasons of summer (June to August) and winter (December to March). You'll have a better chance of finding accommodation and enjoying popular attractions without long lines or crowds.

## Whale Watching:
If your itinerary includes whale watching, the best time to visit Maui is during the winter months (December to April), when humpback whales migrate to warmer waters to breed and give birth. However, even in the off-season you can catch glimpses of whales moving to and from their feeding grounds.

## Surfing and Water Activities:
Surfing conditions on Maui vary throughout the year. Winter months bring big waves to the north coast, while summer months offer quieter

environments for snorkeling, swimming and other water activities. Spring and fall provide a good balance for both surfers and beachgoers, with more stable weather and fewer crowds.

**Events and Festivals:**
Maui hosts a variety of cultural events and festivals throughout the year, including the Maui Film Festival in June, the Maui County Fair in September, and various cultural celebrations and hula festivals. Checking the event calendar can help you plan your visit around these special occasions.

The best time to visit Maui depends on your preferences for weather, crowds, and activities. Whether you're seeking whale watching, surfing, hiking, or simply relaxing on the beach, Maui offers something for every traveler year-round. Just be sure to book accommodations and activities in advance, especially if you plan to visit during the peak tourist season.

# Entry Requirements and Visas

Entry requirements and visa regulations for visiting Maui, as part of Hawaii, depend on your nationality and the purpose of your visit. Here's what you need to know to help you plan your trip:

## United States Citizens:

If you are a citizen of the United States, you do not need a visa to travel to Maui or any other part of Hawaii. As a U.S. citizen, you only need to present a valid U.S. passport or other accepted forms of identification when traveling domestically. This means you can freely enter and stay in Maui without any visa requirements.

## Foreign Visitors:

If you are not a U.S. citizen, you may need to obtain a visa to enter the United States, including Hawaii. The specific visa requirements vary depending on your country of citizenship and the purpose of your visit. The U.S. Department of State has different visa categories for various purposes such as tourism, business, study, and work.

## Visa Waiver Program (VWP):

Citizens of countries participating in the Visa Waiver Program (VWP) may be eligible to travel to the United States for tourism or business purposes for up to 90 days without obtaining a visa. However, they must obtain an approved Electronic System for Travel Authorization (ESTA) before traveling. The ESTA application must be completed online, and approval is usually granted within minutes or hours. Travelers should apply for ESTA well in advance of their planned trip to Maui.

## Non-VWP Countries:

Citizens of countries not participating in the Visa Waiver Program must apply for a nonimmigrant visa at the nearest U.S. embassy or consulate before traveling to Maui. The type of visa required will depend on the purpose of the visit, such as tourism, business, study, or work. Visa applicants will need to complete the appropriate application forms, pay the required fees, and attend an in-person visa interview at the embassy or consulate.

## Customs and Immigration:

Upon arrival in Maui, all travelers, including U.S. citizens, will need to pass through customs and immigration control. Be prepared to present your travel documents, including your passport, visa (if required), and any additional documentation requested by immigration officials. Customs officers may also inspect your luggage and ask questions about the purpose of your visit, the duration of your stay, and any items you are bringing into the country.

Consider purchasing travel insurance to protect against unexpected events that may disrupt your travel plans. By being well-prepared and informed, you can ensure a smooth and enjoyable experience during your visit to the beautiful island of Maui.

# Budgeting and Currency

Budgeting for a trip to Maui involves considering various expenses, including accommodation, transportation, meals, activities, and souvenirs. Here's a typical costs and the currency used in Maui:

## Accommodation:

Accommodation options in Maui range from budget-friendly hostels and vacation rentals to luxury resorts and hotels. Prices vary depending on the location, time of year, and type of accommodation. On average, budget travelers can expect to spend around **$100** to **$200** per night for a basic hotel room or vacation rental, while luxury resorts can cost upwards of **$300** to **$500** or more per night.

## Transportation:

Renting a car is a popular option for exploring Maui, as it provides the flexibility to visit remote areas and attractions at your own pace. Car rental prices vary depending on the type of vehicle and rental duration but typically range from **$50** to **$150** per day. Alternatively, visitors can use public transportation, such as buses, shuttles, and taxis, which offer more affordable options for getting around the island.

## Meals:

Dining options in Maui include a wide range of restaurants, cafes, food trucks, and markets offering diverse cuisines to suit every budget. Prices for meals vary depending on the type of establishment and the mealtime. On average, expect to spend around **$15** to **$30** per person for a meal at a casual restaurant or food truck, while dining at upscale restaurants may cost **$50** or more per person.

## Activities:

Maui offers a wealth of outdoor activities and attractions, including snorkeling, hiking, surfing, zip-lining, and helicopter tours. Prices for activities vary widely, with some being free or low-cost (such as hiking in national parks), while others can be more expensive (such as guided tours or water sports). It's a good idea to research activity prices in advance and budget accordingly.

### Souvenirs and Miscellaneous Expenses:
Don't forget to budget for souvenirs, gifts, and miscellaneous expenses such as entrance fees, parking fees, and tips. Prices for souvenirs vary depending on the item and where you purchase it, so it's a good idea to set aside some extra cash for unexpected expenses.

### Currency:
The currency used in Maui, as part of the United States, is the United States Dollar (USD). Credit cards are widely accepted at most establishments, but it's a good idea to carry some cash for small purchases and places that may not accept cards. ATMs are available in major towns and tourist areas for withdrawing cash if needed.

When budgeting for your trip to Maui, it's essential to research prices, plan ahead, and consider your individual preferences and priorities. By creating a realistic budget and sticking to it, you can enjoy your time in Maui without breaking the bank.

# Packing Tips

Packing for a trip to Maui requires careful consideration of the island's climate, activities, and cultural norms. Here are some essential packing tips to ensure you have everything you need for a comfortable and enjoyable stay:

### Lightweight Clothing:
Pack lightweight, breathable clothing suitable for warm tropical weather. Opt for cotton or moisture-wicking fabrics that will keep you cool and comfortable during your stay. Essentials include shorts, T-shirts, sundresses, swimsuits, and sandals.

### Sun Protection:
Protect yourself from the sun's rays by packing sunscreen with a high SPF, sunglasses, a

wide-brimmed hat, and lightweight clothing that covers your skin. Maui's sun can be strong, especially near the equator, so it's essential to take precautions to avoid sunburn and heat exhaustion.

### Waterproof Gear:
If you plan to spend time at the beach or engage in water activities, consider packing waterproof gear such as a waterproof phone case, dry bag for your belongings, and reef-safe sunscreen to protect the marine environment.

### Hiking Gear:
If you're planning to explore Maui's scenic trails and national parks, pack sturdy hiking shoes or boots, lightweight breathable clothing, a hat, sunglasses, and plenty of water. Additionally, consider bringing a daypack, trail map, insect repellent, and a first-aid kit for emergencies.

### Swimwear and Snorkeling Gear:
Don't forget to pack your swimsuit and any snorkeling gear you may have, such as a mask,

snorkel, and fins. While some rental shops offer snorkeling gear, bringing your own can save you time and ensure a proper fit.

### Casual Evening Attire:

While Maui is known for its laid-back atmosphere, you may want to pack some casual evening attire for dining out or attending cultural events. Lightweight dresses, linen shirts, and comfortable footwear are suitable for most restaurants and nightlife spots.

### Reusable Water Bottle:

Stay hydrated while exploring Maui by bringing a reusable water bottle. Tap water in Maui is safe to drink, so you can refill your bottle at water stations throughout the island to reduce waste and save money on bottled water.

### Travel Essentials:

Don't forget to pack essential travel items such as travel-sized toiletries, medications, travel adapters, chargers, a camera or smartphone for capturing memories, and a travel guide or map of Maui.

## Respectful Attire:
When visiting cultural sites or attending traditional events, it's important to dress respectfully. Pack lightweight, modest clothing that covers your shoulders and knees out of respect for Hawaiian culture and customs.

## Travel Documents:
Finally, don't forget to pack all necessary travel documents, including your passport, travel insurance information, flight tickets, hotel reservations, and any required visas or entry documents.

By packing thoughtfully and preparing for Maui's climate and activities, you can ensure a comfortable and enjoyable trip to this beautiful island paradise.

# Chapter 3: Getting to Maui

*Start your adventure to Maui! Explore different modes of transportation and the necessary documents needed to access this beautiful island in the Pacific.*

## Transportation Options (Airports, Airlines)

Maui has multiple airports, with Kahului Airport (OGG) being the main entry point to the island. It offers a range of domestic and international flights and serves as a central hub for inter-island travel within Hawaii. The airport provides various transportation options such as car rentals, shuttles, taxis, and public transport to reach your destination on Maui. Airlines serving Kahului Airport include Hawaiian Airlines, Alaska Airlines, American Airlines, Delta Air Lines, and Southwest Airlines.

Apart from Kahului Airport, there are other airports on Maui like Kapalua Airport (JHM) and Hana Airport (HNM) that primarily cater to inter-island flights operated by smaller airlines. In terms of transportation within Maui, options include car rentals, shuttle services to major resort areas, taxi services, rideshare options like Uber and Lyft, and the affordable Maui Bus system for travel around the island.

Visitors to Maui can choose from a variety of transportation options, including flights to Kahului Airport and other local airports, along with car rentals, shuttles, taxis, rideshare services, and public transportation for exploring the island.

## Getting Around Maui (Car Rentals, Public Transportation, Tours)

Exploring Maui offers a range of transportation options to cater to different preferences and budgets. Here are the main ways to navigate the island:

## Renting a Car:

Renting a car is a popular option for exploring Maui, providing flexibility to travel at your own pace. Numerous car rental companies are available at Kahului Airport and around the island, offering various vehicles to match your needs and budget. It's advisable to reserve your rental car in advance, especially during busy times, to secure availability and competitive rates. Stay cautious while driving on Maui's narrow and winding roads, especially on popular routes like the Road to Hana and the scenic coastline.

## Public Transportation - Maui Bus:

The Maui Bus system offers affordable transportation between major towns and attractions on the island. The bus covers much of Maui, including Kahului, Lahaina, Kihei, and Wailea, making it a convenient choice for budget-conscious travelers. Bus schedules and routes can be found online or at the Maui Bus Transit Center in Kahului. While the bus serves many popular spots, it may not be as frequent or convenient as having your own transport.

## Shuttle Services:
Various shuttle companies offer transportation between Kahului Airport and major resort areas like Lahaina, Kaanapali, Kihei, and Wailea. These services include shared or private options, providing door-to-door transfers to your accommodation. It's wise to book in advance, especially during busy periods, to ensure availability and timely pickups.

## Taxis and Rideshare:
Taxis and rideshare services like Uber and Lyft are accessible on Maui, offering convenient transport for short trips or when without a rental car. Taxis can be hailed at designated stands at places like airports, resorts, and major towns. Rideshare services work similarly to elsewhere, letting you request rides through an app and pay electronically.

## Guided Tours:

For those who prefer guided experiences, numerous tour companies offer guided tours to explore Maui's attractions. These tours span from sightseeing and snorkeling trips to whale watching and adventure tours, providing opportunities to learn from guides, mingle with other travelers, and maximize your time on the island.

Whether you opt for renting a car, using public transport, booking shuttles, or joining guided tours, Maui offers plenty of ways to get around and enjoy all it has to offer. Select the mode of transportation that aligns with your travel style, budget, and itinerary, and savor your adventure on the Valley Isle.

# Month by Month Weather in Maui

Maui enjoys a mild and pleasant climate year-round, characterized by warm temperatures, sunny skies, and refreshing trade winds. However, there are slight variations in weather patterns from month to month. Here's a month-by-month weather in Maui:

## January:

January is one of the coolest months in Maui, with average temperatures ranging from 63°F to 81°F (17°C to 27°C). While it's generally sunny and dry, there may be occasional showers, particularly in the windward (northeastern) areas of the island. January is a popular time for whale watching, as humpback whales migrate to Maui's warm waters to breed and give birth.

## February:

Similar to January, February brings mild temperatures and relatively dry conditions to Maui. Average temperatures range from 63°F to 81°F (17°C to 27°C), making it an ideal time for outdoor activities such as hiking, snorkeling, and surfing. Whale watching continues to be a highlight of the month, with ample opportunities to see these majestic creatures up close.

## March:

March marks the transition to warmer temperatures in Maui, with average highs reaching 82°F (28°C). While the weather remains sunny and pleasant, there may be increased rainfall as the island transitions from the winter to the spring season. March is an excellent time to explore Maui's lush landscapes and blooming flora, including the famous jacaranda trees in Upcountry Maui.

## April:

April brings warmer temperatures and drier conditions to Maui, with average highs reaching 83°F (28°C). The island experiences plenty of sunshine, making it an ideal time for beach activities, snorkeling, and swimming. April is also a popular month for outdoor events and festivals, including cultural celebrations and the annual Maui County Agricultural Festival.

## May:

May is one of the sunniest months in Maui, with average temperatures ranging from 66°F to 85°F (19°C to 29°C). The weather is warm and dry, perfect for exploring Maui's outdoor attractions, hiking trails, and scenic viewpoints. May is also a great time for water activities such as snorkeling, diving, and sailing.

## June:

June marks the beginning of summer in Maui, with average temperatures ranging from 68°F to 87°F (20°C to 31°C). The weather is warm and sunny, with occasional afternoon showers in some areas of the island. June is an excellent time for beachgoers and water sports enthusiasts, as ocean conditions are generally calm and inviting.

## July:

July is one of the warmest months in Maui, with average highs reaching 88°F (31°C). The weather is hot and sunny, perfect for spending long days at the beach or exploring Maui's scenic coastline. July is also a popular time for outdoor activities such as hiking, zip-lining, and horseback riding.

## August:

August brings similar weather conditions to July, with hot temperatures and plenty of sunshine. Average highs reach 88°F (31°C), making it one of the warmest months of the year in Maui. While there may be occasional afternoon showers, August is generally a great time for outdoor adventures and water activities.

## September:

September marks the transition to the fall season in Maui, with slightly cooler temperatures and increased chances of rainfall. Average highs range from 87°F to 88°F (31°C to 31°C), and the island experiences fewer crowds compared to the summer months. September is a good time to visit if you prefer quieter beaches and hiking trails.

## October:

October brings mild temperatures and pleasant weather to Maui, with average highs ranging from 84°F to 87°F (29°C to 31°C). While there may be occasional showers, October is generally a sunny and dry month, ideal for outdoor activities such as snorkeling, surfing, and hiking. October is also a popular time for cultural events and festivals on the island.

## November:

November marks the transition to the winter season in Maui, with slightly cooler temperatures and increased rainfall. Average highs range from 81°F to 85°F (27°C to 29°C), and the island experiences more frequent afternoon showers. November is still a great time to visit Maui, with fewer crowds and opportunities to experience authentic Hawaiian culture and traditions.

## December:

December brings mild temperatures and sunny skies to Maui, with average highs ranging from 78°F to 82°F (26°C to 28°C). While there may be occasional showers, December is generally a pleasant month for outdoor activities and beachgoers. December is also a popular time for holiday celebrations and festive events on the island.

Maui enjoys beautiful weather year-round, making it a fantastic destination for travelers seeking sun, sand, and adventure in every season. Whether you visit during the warm summer months or the mild winter season, Maui's natural beauty and vibrant culture are sure to leave a lasting impression.

# Chapter 4: Accommodations in Maui

*Uncover your second home in Maui! Check out a range of lodging options, from extravagant resorts to comfortable vacation homes.*

# Types of Accommodations (Hotels, Resorts, Vacation Rentals)

Maui provides a wide variety of accommodation options to cater to the preferences and budgets of all travelers. The main types of accommodations available on the island include:

### Hotels and Resorts:

Maui boasts a range of hotels and resorts, from luxurious beachfront properties to budget-friendly options, each offering amenities like pools, restaurants, and concierge services.

### Vacation Rentals:

Visitors can opt for vacation homes, villas, condos, and apartments for more space and flexibility during their stay, with amenities such as kitchens, living areas, and Wi-Fi.

### Bed and Breakfasts (B&Bs):

Cozy B&Bs on Maui offer personalized service, homemade breakfasts, and a chance to connect with local hosts and fellow travelers in charming settings.

### Hostels and Budget Accommodations:

Backpackers and budget-conscious travelers can choose from hostels with dormitory-style rooms or shared facilities for an affordable stay.

### Luxury Retreats and Private Estates:

Travelers looking for luxury can indulge in upscale retreats and private estates with lavish amenities, stunning views, and dedicated staff.

<u>**Camping and Glamping:**</u>
Adventurous travelers can immerse themselves in Maui's natural beauty by camping or glamping in scenic areas with options ranging from tent sites to luxurious safari tents and eco-friendly cottages.

Maui offers a diverse array of accommodations to cater to various travel preferences, whether looking for luxury, affordability, or an immersive natural experience.

# Areas to Stay in Maui (Beachfront, Towns, Rural Areas)

Maui offers a variety of distinct areas to stay, each with its own unique charm, attractions, and atmosphere. Here are some of the main areas to consider when choosing accommodations on the island:

## Wailea and Makena:

Located on Maui's sunny southern coast, Wailea and Makena are known for their upscale resorts, pristine beaches, and world-class golf courses. This area boasts luxurious accommodations, fine dining restaurants, and upscale shopping centers. Visitors can enjoy activities such as snorkeling, stand-up paddleboarding, and sunset cruises.

## Kihei:

Situated just north of Wailea, Kihei offers a more laid-back atmosphere with a range of accommodations, from budget-friendly condos to beachfront resorts. Kihei's beaches are popular for swimming, snorkeling, and sunbathing, and the town has a vibrant nightlife scene with bars, restaurants, and live music venues.

## Lahaina and Kaanapali:

Located on Maui's west coast, Lahaina and Kaanapali are historic areas known for their picturesque beaches, lively waterfront, and cultural attractions. Lahaina's Front Street is lined with shops, galleries, and restaurants housed in historic buildings, while Kaanapali boasts luxurious resorts, championship golf courses, and the iconic Black Rock snorkeling spot.

## Napili and Kapalua:

North of Kaanapali, Napili and Kapalua offer a more secluded and scenic retreat with stunning beaches, lush landscapes, and championship golf courses. This area is known for its upscale resorts, luxury villas, and world-class dining options. Visitors can enjoy activities such as hiking, snorkeling, and whale watching during the winter months.

## Paia and Upcountry Maui:

Located on Maui's north shore, Paia is a charming town known for its bohemian vibe, eclectic shops, and art galleries. Upcountry Maui, situated inland, offers a cooler climate, rolling hills, and panoramic views of the island. Accommodations in this area include bed and breakfasts, vacation rentals, and boutique hotels, providing a peaceful retreat away from the tourist crowds.

### Hana:

Located on Maui's remote eastern coast, Hana is a secluded and scenic area known for its rugged landscapes, lush rainforests, and cultural heritage. Accommodations in Hana range from rustic cabins and eco-lodges to luxury resorts, offering a peaceful retreat surrounded by natural beauty. Visitors can explore attractions such as the Road to Hana, Wai'anapanapa State Park, and the Seven Sacred Pools.

### Rural Areas and Beachfront Retreats:

Throughout Maui, visitors can find rural areas and beachfront retreats offering secluded accommodations and a tranquil atmosphere. These areas provide a peaceful escape from the tourist crowds, with options such as vacation rentals, cottages, and eco-friendly resorts nestled along Maui's coastline or in rural settings.

Whether you prefer a luxurious beachfront resort, a charming town with shops and restaurants, or a secluded retreat surrounded by nature, Maui offers a diverse range of areas to stay that cater to every traveler's preferences and interests.

## Booking Tips and Recommendations

To have a smooth and enjoyable trip to Maui, consider these tips:

### Secure Accommodations Early:
Maui is a popular destination, especially in peak seasons like summer and winter. Book accommodations like hotels or vacation rentals several months in advance for the best rates.

### Compare Prices and Amenities:
Research online for the best deals that meet your needs and budget. Look at location, amenities, and cancellation policies when deciding.

**Prioritize Location and Accessibility:**
Choose accommodations close to the attractions you want to visit. Consider access to restaurants, shopping, and transportation.

**Be Flexible with Dates:**
Travel during off-peak or mid-week periods for lower prices and fewer crowds. Spring and fall might be more affordable.

**Look for Special Deals:**
Check for promotions from hotels that may offer discounts, freebies, or activity packages. Stay informed through newsletters or loyalty programs.

**Check Reviews:**
Read reviews on sites like TripAdvisor to learn about the quality and service of accommodations from other travelers.

## Consider Travel Insurance:

Protect your trip investment with insurance in case of unforeseen events like flight cancellations or emergencies.

## Plan Activities Early:

Book popular activities like snorkeling or luaus in advance to ensure availability. Research tour operators and read reviews before booking.

By following these tips, you can have a stress-free and memorable trip to Maui with the accommodations and experiences you desire.

# Chapter 5: Must-See Attractions in Maui

*Discover the unforgettable highlights of Maui! Explore the stunning attractions of the island, including the famous Road to Hana and the majestic Haleakalā.*

## Top Beaches (Ka'anapali, Wailea, Hana)

Maui is renowned for its stunning beaches, each offering unique landscapes, crystal-clear waters, and opportunities for water activities and relaxation. Here are some of the top beaches in Maui, including those in Ka'anapali, Wailea, and Hana:

### Ka'anapali Beach:
Located on Maui's west coast, Ka'anapali Beach is one of the island's most famous and beloved beaches. This three-mile stretch of golden sand is fringed by palm trees and bordered by a scenic

oceanfront walkway known as the Ka'anapali Beachwalk.

Ka'anapali Beach offers excellent swimming and snorkeling conditions, with calm waters and vibrant coral reefs just offshore. Visitors can also enjoy beachfront dining, shopping, and entertainment at the nearby Whalers Village shopping center.

Popular activities at Ka'anapali Beach include sunset cruises, parasailing, stand-up paddleboarding, and beach volleyball. The beach is also known for its iconic cliff-diving ceremony at Pu'u Keka'a (Black Rock) each evening.

### Wailea Beach:

Situated in the upscale resort area of Wailea, Wailea Beach is a pristine and picturesque stretch of golden sand overlooking the turquoise waters of the Pacific Ocean. This crescent-shaped beach is backed by luxury resorts, lush landscaping, and manicured lawns.

Wailea Beach is ideal for swimming, sunbathing, and snorkeling, with calm waters and excellent visibility for observing marine life. Visitors can rent beach chairs, umbrellas, and water sports equipment from beach attendants or nearby rental shops.

The beachfront promenade at Wailea offers stunning views of the coastline and is perfect for leisurely strolls or jogging. Nearby, visitors can explore upscale shopping centers, world-class golf courses, and fine dining restaurants in the Wailea Resort area.

### Hamoa Beach (Near Hana):
Located on Maui's remote eastern coast near the town of Hana, Hamoa Beach is a hidden gem known for its natural beauty and seclusion. This crescent-shaped beach is surrounded by lush cliffs, swaying palm trees, and turquoise waters, creating a postcard-perfect setting.

Hamoa Beach is popular for swimming, bodysurfing, and sunbathing, with gentle waves and soft golden sand. The beach's offshore reef provides protection from strong currents, making it suitable for visitors of all ages.

To reach Hamoa Beach, visitors can take the scenic Road to Hana, a winding coastal highway known for its breathtaking views and iconic landmarks. While the journey may be long and challenging, the reward of discovering Hamoa Beach's untouched beauty is well worth the effort.

These are one of the top beaches in Maui, each offering its own unique charm and attractions for visitors to enjoy. Whether you're seeking relaxation, adventure, or natural beauty, Maui's beaches provide endless opportunities for unforgettable experiences in paradise.

# Natural Wonders (Haleakalā National Park, Road to Hana)

Maui is home to several natural wonders that showcase the island's breathtaking landscapes, diverse ecosystems, and rich cultural heritage. Two standout attractions are Haleakalā National Park and the Road to Hana:

## Haleakalā National Park:

Haleakalā, meaning "House of the Sun" in Hawaiian, is a dormant volcano that forms the centerpiece of Haleakalā National Park. The park encompasses over 33,000 acres of protected wilderness, including the summit crater, lush rainforests, and subalpine desert landscapes.

The main highlight of Haleakalā National Park is the stunning sunrise or sunset views from the summit of Haleakalā Volcano, which stands at over 10,000 feet above sea level. Visitors can drive or hike to the summit to witness the breathtaking spectacle of the sun rising or setting above the clouds.

Haleakalā National Park offers a network of hiking trails for all skill levels, ranging from short nature walks to challenging multi-day backpacking adventures. Popular hikes include the Sliding Sands Trail, Pipiwai Trail, and Halemau'u Trail, which showcase the park's diverse ecosystems, native flora, and wildlife.

<u>**Road to Hana:**</u>
The Road to Hana is a scenic coastal highway that winds its way along Maui's rugged eastern coastline, offering travelers breathtaking views of waterfalls, lush rainforests, dramatic sea cliffs, and pristine beaches. The road stretches for approximately 64 miles from the town of Kahului to the remote village of Hana.

Along the Road to Hana, visitors can explore numerous natural attractions and landmarks, including the Twin Falls, Wailua Falls, Bamboo Forest, and Seven Sacred Pools (Ohe'o Gulch) in Haleakalā National Park's Kīpahulu District.

The Road to Hana is also known for its numerous roadside fruit stands, scenic overlooks, and cultural sites, providing opportunities to learn about Hawaiian history, traditions, and local culture. Travelers can immerse themselves in the natural beauty and tranquility of Maui's eastern coast while experiencing the spirit of aloha.

These natural wonders are just a glimpse of the awe-inspiring landscapes and experiences awaiting visitors to Maui. Whether you're exploring the summit of Haleakalā or embarking on a scenic drive along the Road to Hana, Maui's natural beauty and cultural heritage are sure to leave a lasting impression.

## Cultural Sites (Lahaina, Iao Valley State Park, Maui Ocean Center)

Maui is rich in cultural heritage and boasts several notable sites that offer insight into the island's history, traditions, and natural wonders.

Here are three cultural sites in Maui worth exploring:

## Lahaina Historic District:

Lahaina, located on Maui's west coast, is a historic town that served as a thriving whaling port and capital of the Hawaiian Kingdom in the 19th century. Today, Lahaina's charming streets are lined with historic buildings, museums, art galleries, and shops, offering visitors a glimpse into its colorful past.

The Lahaina Historic District is home to several significant cultural sites, including the Baldwin Home Museum, Hale Pa'ahao (Old Lahaina Prison), and Wo Hing Museum & Cookhouse. Visitors can take self-guided walking tours or join guided tours to learn about Lahaina's history, architecture, and cultural significance.

Lahaina's Front Street is a bustling hub of activity, with restaurants, bars, and shops housed in restored buildings dating back to the whaling era. The Lahaina Banyan Court Park, home to a massive banyan tree planted in 1873, is a popular gathering spot for locals and visitors alike.

## Iao Valley State Park:

Located in Central Maui, Iao Valley State Park is a lush and verdant valley known for its towering emerald peaks, cascading waterfalls, and rich cultural history. The park is home to the iconic Iao Needle, a natural rock formation that rises 1,200 feet above the valley floor.

Iao Valley has great significance in Hawaiian history and culture, serving as a sacred burial ground for Hawaiian ali'i (royalty) and a place of spiritual importance. Visitors can explore the park's botanical gardens, scenic trails, and historic sites while learning about its cultural significance.

The Iao Valley State Park offers opportunities for hiking, picnicking, and wildlife viewing amidst its lush rainforest setting. Interpretive displays and educational programs provide insight into the valley's geological features, native plants, and traditional Hawaiian practices.

## Maui Ocean Center:

Located in Ma'alaea, the Maui Ocean Center is a state-of-the-art aquarium and marine science center that showcases the marine life and ecosystems of Hawaii and the Pacific. The center features interactive exhibits, educational programs, and live animal displays, offering visitors a unique opportunity to learn about Hawaii's underwater world.

The Maui Ocean Center highlights the importance of marine conservation and stewardship, with exhibits focusing on coral reefs, sea turtles, sharks, and other marine species found in Hawaiian waters. Visitors can explore indoor and outdoor exhibits, including the Open Ocean exhibit with a 750,000-gallon saltwater aquarium.

The Maui Ocean Center also offers behind-the-scenes tours, animal encounters, and educational programs for visitors of all ages. It serves as a valuable resource for learning about Hawaii's marine environment and the efforts to protect and preserve it for future generations.

These cultural sites in Maui offer immersive experiences that celebrate the island's history, traditions, and natural beauty. Whether exploring the historic streets of Lahaina, marveling at the majestic Iao Needle, or discovering the wonders of Hawaii's marine life at the Maui Ocean Center, visitors to Maui can gain a deeper appreciation for the island's rich cultural heritage.

# Chapter 6: Outdoor Adventures in Maui

*Experience exciting outdoor adventures in Maui! Whether it's snorkeling at Molokini or exploring dense rainforests through hiking, there are plenty of thrilling activities waiting for you on the island.*

## Snorkeling and Diving Spots

Maui is famous for its rich marine life and provides some of the finest snorkeling and diving locations in Hawaii. Here are some top spots for snorkeling and diving in Maui:

### Molokini Crater:
Situated off South Maui's coast, Molokini Crater is a crescent-shaped volcanic crater that can be reached via a short boat ride from Ma'alaea Harbor or Kihei. This marine sanctuary boasts clear waters, vibrant coral reefs, and a variety of marine creatures like tropical fish, sea turtles, and reef sharks. Explorers can discover coral

gardens, rock formations, and underwater caves within the crater.

## Turtle Town:
Turtle Town on Maui's southern coast is well-known for its abundance of green sea turtles. Snorkelers can witness these gentle creatures in their natural habitat at sites like Maluaka Beach in Makena and Pu'u Olai Beach Park in Wailea, by maintaining a respectful distance.

## Honolua Bay:
Positioned near Kapalua on Maui's northwest coast, Honolua Bay features pristine coral reefs and a diverse marine ecosystem. Protected from powerful winds, this marine reserve offers clear waters and a range of marine life such as colorful fish, eels, and octopuses.

## Black Rock (Pu'u Keka'a):
Black Rock at the end of Ka'anapali Beach provides calm waters and abundant marine species like colorful fish, sea turtles, eagle rays,

and reef sharks. This iconic spot is favorable for snorkeling, diving, and watching the nightly cliff diving ceremony.

## Coral Gardens (Olowalu):
Off Olowalu Beach on Maui's west coast lies Coral Gardens, a colorful reef filled with marine life such as coral species, reef fish, sea turtles, and occasional sightings of manta rays and whale sharks in winter. Easily accessible by boat or kayak, this site offers ideal conditions for snorkeling and diving.

These top spots in Maui offer unique underwater adventures and opportunities to see Hawaii's diverse marine life. From swimming with sea turtles to exploring coral reefs, Maui's waters provide memorable experiences for snorkelers and divers of all levels.

# Hiking Trails

Maui provides a range of hiking trails suitable for all skill levels, from easy strolls to demanding treks through vibrant rainforests and volcanic terrains. Here are some prominent hiking routes in Maui:

## Haleakalā Crater Trails:

### Sliding Sands Trail:
An 11-mile round-trip path in Haleakalā National Park that descends into the Haleakalā Volcano crater, showcasing breathtaking views of colorful cinder cones and the crater floor.

### Halemau'u Trail:
This 7-mile round-trip trail in Haleakalā National Park skirts the crater rim, presenting panoramic vistas and chances to spot endemic plants like silversword and indigenous nēnē geese.

## Iao Valley State Park Trails:

### Iao Needle Lookout Trail:
A short paved trail leading to a lookout point for the incredible Iao Needle rock formation towering over the valley.

### Iao Valley Stream Loop Trail:
An easy 0.6-mile loop trail offering a stroll through lush rainforest and by the soothing Iao Stream.

### Waihe'e Ridge Trail:
A moderately challenging 4.5-mile round-trip hike in West Maui with stunning views of Waihe'e Valley and the coast, passing through lush rainforest with streams and waterfalls.

### Pipiwai Trail:
A 4-mile round-trip hike in Haleakalā National Park's Kīpahulu District leading to the magnificent Waimoku Falls, taking hikers through bamboo forests and past banyan trees.

## Twin Falls Trail:

A brief and easy hike along the Road to Hana culminating in a picturesque waterfall and swimming area.

## Hosmer Grove Trail:

A short nature loop trail in Haleakalā National Park provides easy walking and birdwatching amidst a forest of native and introduced trees.

## La Perouse Bay Trail:

A rugged coastal hike in South Maui passes through ancient lava fields to reach La Perouse Bay, where historic village ruins and wildlife sightings can be enjoyed.

These trails showcase the diverse landscapes of Maui and offer unique experiences for hikers. Always ensure to check trail conditions, weather forecasts, and adhere to park regulations, following Leave No Trace guidelines to preserve the environment.

## Water Activities (Surfing, Windsurfing, Stand-Up Paddleboarding)

Maui's warm waters and consistent trade winds make it a great place for a variety of water activities like surfing, windsurfing, and stand-up paddleboarding. Here's a look at each activity and some top spots to enjoy them on the island:

### Surfing:
Maui is famous for its excellent surfing conditions catering to all skill levels. Whether you're a beginner or an expert, Maui has diverse surf spots to choose from.

### Top Surf Spots:
Ho'okipa Beach Park for experienced surfers, Honolua Bay for intermediate to advanced surfers, and Lahaina Breakwall for beginners.

### Windsurfing:
Maui is known as a top windsurfing destination globally due to its consistent trade winds. Enthusiasts come to experience its challenging waves.

## Popular Windsurfing Spots:
Ho'okipa Beach Park, Kanaha Beach Park, and Spreckelsville Beach are popular spots offering varied conditions.

## Stand-Up Paddleboarding (SUP):
Stand-up paddleboarding is increasingly popular in Maui for its accessibility and versatility, offering a unique way to explore the coastline.

## Popular SUP Spots:
Napili Bay, Kapalua Bay, Makena Landing, and Maliko Gulch are popular spots known for calm waters and encounters with marine life.

From surfers to windsurfers to paddleboarders, Maui provides endless opportunities for water activities catering to all interests and skill levels. Remember to stay safe, follow regulations, and enjoy Maui's ocean playground responsibly.

# Chapter 7: Dining and Cuisine in Maui

*Enjoy the tastes of Maui! Treat yourself to the delicious seafood, exotic fruits, and a variety of dishes that highlight the island's culinary treasures.*

# Local Hawaiian Cuisine

Hawaiian cuisine is a unique blend of flavors and influences from various cultures, including Native Hawaiian, Polynesian, Asian, and Western cuisines. Here are some iconic dishes and ingredients that define local Hawaiian cuisine:

## Poke:

Poke (pronounced poh-kay) is a traditional Hawaiian dish made with cubed raw fish (often ahi tuna or salmon) marinated in a flavorful mixture of soy sauce, sesame oil, green onions, and other seasonings. It is typically served as an appetizer or snack and can be found at local markets, grocery stores, and restaurants throughout Hawaii.

## Kalua Pig:

Kalua pig is a classic Hawaiian dish made by slow-cooking a whole pig in an underground oven called an imu. The pig is seasoned with salt and sometimes other spices, then wrapped in ti leaves and banana leaves before being placed in the imu to roast for several hours. The result is tender, smoky, and flavorful pork that is often served at luaus and other special occasions.

## Laulau:

Laulau is a traditional Hawaiian dish consisting of pork, fish, or chicken wrapped in taro leaves and steamed until tender. The meat is often seasoned with salt and sometimes other ingredients like butterfish or pork fat for added flavor. Laulau is a popular dish at luaus and can also be found at local Hawaiian restaurants and food trucks.

## Loco Moco:

Loco moco is a beloved Hawaiian comfort food made with white rice topped with a hamburger patty, a fried egg, and brown gravy. It is often served with sides like macaroni salad or green salad. Loco moco is a hearty and satisfying dish that can be found at diners, cafes, and plate lunch restaurants throughout Hawaii.

## Plate Lunch:

Plate lunch is a popular meal in Hawaii that typically consists of a protein (such as chicken katsu, teriyaki beef, or mahi mahi), two scoops of white rice, and macaroni salad. Plate lunches are served at local eateries, food trucks, and cafes across the islands and are a convenient and affordable option for lunch or dinner.

## Haupia:

Haupia is a traditional Hawaiian dessert made with coconut milk, sugar, and cornstarch. It has a smooth and creamy texture similar to pudding and is often served chilled in squares or cubes.

Haupia is a popular dessert at luaus, potlucks, and other gatherings in Hawaii.

### Malasadas:

Malasadas are Portuguese-inspired fried doughnuts that have become a beloved treat in Hawaii. They are typically made with yeast dough, deep-fried until golden brown, and coated in sugar. Malasadas are often filled with flavored creams or fruit fillings and can be found at bakeries and food trucks throughout the islands.

These are one of the delicious and diverse dishes that make up local Hawaiian cuisine. Whether you're sampling traditional favorites at a local restaurant or enjoying a homemade feast at a Hawaiian luau, Hawaiian cuisine offers a rich and flavorful culinary experience that celebrates the unique cultural heritage of the islands.

# Best Restaurants and Food Trucks

Maui is home to a vibrant culinary scene, with an array of restaurants and food trucks offering delicious and diverse cuisine inspired by local ingredients and flavors. Here are some of the best restaurants and food trucks on the island:

## Best Restaurants:

### Mama's Fish House:
Located in Paia on Maui's North Shore, Mama's Fish House is renowned for its fresh seafood, elegant ambiance, and stunning oceanfront setting. The restaurant sources its fish directly from local fishermen and serves up dishes like seafood curry, stuffed mahi-mahi, and lobster tail in a coconut-ginger sauce.

### Leoda's Kitchen and Pie Shop:
Situated in Olowalu near Lahaina, Leoda's is a charming eatery known for its homemade pies, sandwiches, and comfort food classics. Guests can enjoy savory pies, such as chicken pot pie

and shepherd's pie, as well as sweet pies, including banana cream and macadamia nut chocolate.

## Hula Grill Kaanapali:
Located on Ka'anapali Beach, Hula Grill offers a relaxed beachfront dining experience with a focus on fresh, locally sourced ingredients and Hawaiian-inspired cuisine. Diners can savor dishes like macadamia nut-crusted mahi-mahi, kalua pork tacos, and coconut shrimp while enjoying panoramic ocean views.

## Merriman's Maui:
Situated in Kapalua, Merriman's showcases farm-to-table cuisine highlighting the flavors of Hawaii's land and sea. The restaurant offers a seasonal menu featuring dishes like seared ahi poke, grilled local fish, and grass-fed beef served with locally grown produce and artisanal ingredients.

## Star Noodle:

Located in Lahaina, Star Noodle serves up inventive Asian fusion cuisine in a hip and casual setting. Guests can enjoy a variety of noodle dishes, small plates, and shared plates inspired by Japanese, Chinese, and Filipino culinary traditions, along with craft cocktails and sake.

## Best Food Trucks:

## Geste Shrimp Truck:

This popular food truck is often found parked along the Hana Highway near Kahului. Geste Shrimp Truck serves up delicious garlic butter shrimp plates and shrimp tacos, featuring locally sourced shrimp and flavorful sauces.

## Horhito's Mobile Taqueria:

Horhito's is a beloved food truck serving authentic Mexican cuisine, including tacos, burritos, and quesadillas. The truck often sets up shop in various locations around Maui, offering tasty and affordable options for a quick bite.

## Three's Bar & Grill Food Truck:

Three's Bar & Grill, located in Kihei, operates a food truck that serves up creative and flavorful dishes inspired by Hawaiian, Pacific Rim, and Southwestern cuisines. The truck offers a rotating menu of tacos, sliders, and poke bowls, along with refreshing drinks and desserts.

## The Fish Market Maui:

Located in Lahaina, The Fish Market Maui offers fresh seafood dishes served from a food truck parked near Lahaina Harbor. Guests can enjoy poke bowls, fish tacos, fish and chips, and other seafood specialties made with locally caught fish.

## Da Nani Pirates:

This food truck, located in Wailuku, offers a variety of hearty and satisfying dishes inspired by Hawaiian and Filipino cuisines. Da Nani Pirates serves up favorites like loco moco, garlic shrimp plates, and chicken adobo, along with sides like macaroni salad and rice.

These are one of the best restaurants and food trucks on Maui, each offering unique flavors, ambiance, and dining experiences that reflect the island's diverse culinary landscape. Whether you're craving fresh seafood, innovative fusion cuisine, or authentic street food, Maui has something to satisfy every palate.

## Dining Etiquette and Tips

To have a pleasant dining experience in Maui, it's important to understand and respect local customs and etiquette. Here are some tips to keep in mind:

Make reservations in advance, especially for popular restaurants or during busy times.

Be on time for your reservation or arrive within a reasonable timeframe.

Check for any specific dress codes at the restaurant you plan to visit.

Remember to tip appropriately, as gratuity is usually not included in the bill.

Show respect for local customs, especially the aloha spirit of kindness and hospitality.

When ordering, communicate politely with your server, and ask about any dietary restrictions.

Embrace the idea of sharing food, as communal dining is valued in Hawaiian culture.

End your meal with a genuine thank you, such as saying "**mahalo**" to the staff.

Take your time to relax and enjoy your meal in the leisurely atmosphere of Maui.

By following these tips, you can make the most of your dining experience in Maui and honor the local traditions. Whether you're dining casually or at a fine restaurant, embracing the aloha spirit will ensure a memorable time on the beautiful island of Maui.

# Chapter 8. Cultural Experiences in Maui

*Immerse yourself in the vibrant culture of Maui by delving into Hawaiian traditions, participating in luaus, and visiting cultural landmarks to enhance your island adventure.*

## Luaus and Traditional Performances

Luaus are a popular cultural experience in Maui, offering visitors the opportunity to enjoy traditional Hawaiian food, music, and dance in a festive atmosphere. Here are some of the top luaus and traditional performances in Maui:

### Old Lahaina Luau:

Located in Lahaina, the Old Lahaina Luau is one of the most renowned luaus in Hawaii, known for its authentic cultural experience and breathtaking oceanfront setting. Guests can enjoy a traditional Hawaiian feast, including kalua pig cooked in an imu (underground oven), poi (taro paste), and fresh seafood, while being entertained by hula dancers, musicians, and storytellers.

**Feast at Lele:**
Situated in Lahaina, the Feast at Lele offers a unique culinary journey through the Polynesian islands, with a five-course dinner featuring dishes inspired by Hawaii, Tahiti, Samoa, and New Zealand. Each course is accompanied by traditional music and dance performances representing the different cultures of Polynesia.

**Drums of the Pacific Luau:**
Held at the Hyatt Regency Maui Resort & Spa in Ka'anapali, the Drums of the Pacific Luau is a family-friendly celebration featuring a lavish buffet dinner, including Hawaiian specialties like kalua pork, salmon, and poi, as well as an open bar with tropical cocktails. Guests can enjoy traditional Polynesian music and dance performances, including hula, fire dancing, and Tahitian drumming.

**Royal Lahaina Luau:**

Located at the Royal Lahaina Resort in Ka'anapali, the Royal Lahaina Luau offers a captivating evening of Hawaiian culture and entertainment. Guests can indulge in a buffet dinner featuring local favorites like kalua pork, teriyaki chicken, and fresh island fish, while enjoying live music and dance performances under the stars.

**Te Au Moana Luau:**

Situated at the Wailea Beach Marriott Resort & Spa in Wailea, the Te Au Moana Luau celebrates the rich heritage of Hawaii through food, music, and dance. Guests can feast on a buffet dinner showcasing traditional Hawaiian and Polynesian dishes, while being entertained by hula dancers, musicians, and fire knife performers.

In addition to luaus, visitors to Maui can also enjoy traditional Hawaiian performances and cultural activities at various venues across the island, including hotels, resorts, cultural centers, and shopping malls. These performances often feature hula dancers, ukulele players, and storytellers sharing the history and traditions of Hawaii through music and dance. Whether you're attending a luau or enjoying a cultural performance, experiencing the beauty and spirit of Hawaiian culture is an essential part of any visit to Maui.

## Learning Hawaiian Culture and History

Discovering and understanding Hawaiian culture and history is a valuable experience that can enhance your appreciation of the islands and their inhabitants. Here are some tips for getting immersed in the rich Hawaiian culture and history during your visit to Maui:

Explore cultural landmarks and historical sites like Iao Valley State Park to appreciate the significance of the area in Hawaiian history.

Attend cultural events like hula performances or traditional music concerts to immerse yourself in the local culture.

Join guided cultural tours to learn from local experts about Hawaiian traditions, temples, and historical sites.

Take part in cultural workshops like lei-making or hula dancing to learn traditional arts and crafts.

Dive into books and literature about Hawaiian culture and mythology to deepen your knowledge.

Visit museums and exhibits dedicated to Hawaiian culture and history, such as the Bailey House Museum in Wailuku.

Engage in conversations with locals to gain insights into their experiences and cultural practices.

Show respect for cultural protocols, such as removing shoes before entering sacred sites, to honor traditional customs.

By embracing Hawaiian culture and history, you'll develop a stronger connection to the islands and their people, fostering a sense of aloha that resonates with the land and its heritage.

# Art Galleries and Museums

Maui boasts a vibrant arts and culture scene, with numerous art galleries and museums showcasing the island's rich heritage and creative talent. Here are some notable art galleries and museums to visit while in Maui:

### Hui No'eau Visual Arts Center:
Located in Upcountry Maui, the Hui No'eau Visual Arts Center is a nonprofit arts organization dedicated to promoting artistic expression and education. The center features

rotating exhibitions of contemporary art, traditional crafts, and local artists' works. Visitors can also participate in art classes, workshops, and cultural events.

## Maui Arts & Cultural Center (MACC):
Situated in Kahului, the Maui Arts & Cultural Center is the island's premier cultural venue, hosting a diverse range of performances, exhibitions, and events throughout the year. The center features multiple galleries showcasing visual art, photography, and multimedia installations by local and international artists.

## Schaefer International Gallery:
Located within the Maui Arts & Cultural Center, the Schaefer International Gallery is a spacious exhibition space that hosts rotating art exhibitions highlighting diverse artistic styles and cultural perspectives. The gallery showcases contemporary art, traditional crafts, and multimedia installations from Hawaii and around the world.

## Lahaina Arts Society:
Situated in the historic town of Lahaina, the Lahaina Arts Society operates the Banyan Tree Gallery, a cooperative gallery featuring the works of local Maui artists. Visitors can browse and purchase a wide variety of artwork, including paintings, ceramics, glass art, jewelry, and more, while strolling through Lahaina's bustling waterfront district.

## Maui Hands:
With multiple locations across Maui, Maui Hands is a popular gallery and retail chain specializing in locally made arts and crafts. Each Maui Hands gallery features a curated selection of handmade jewelry, pottery, woodwork, textiles, and other artisanal products created by Maui artists and artisans.

## Bailey House Museum:
Located in Wailuku, the Bailey House Museum is operated by the Maui Historical Society and showcases artifacts, photographs, and exhibits related to Maui's history and cultural heritage.

The museum is housed in a historic missionary-era building and offers guided tours that provide insights into Maui's past.

### Hale Ho'ike'ike at the Bailey House:
Adjacent to the Bailey House Museum, Hale Ho'ike'ike is a cultural center and museum that features exhibits on Hawaiian history, art, and culture. Visitors can explore displays on Hawaiian royalty, ancient artifacts, and traditional crafts, as well as attend cultural events and demonstrations.

These are one of the art galleries and museums that contribute to Maui's vibrant arts and culture scene. Whether you're exploring contemporary art at the Maui Arts & Cultural Center or discovering traditional crafts at the Lahaina Arts Society, Maui offers a wealth of opportunities to immerse yourself in the island's creative spirit and cultural heritage.

# Chapter 9: Shopping in Maui

*Explore the ultimate shopping experience in Maui! Whether you prefer browsing through local markets or shopping at upscale boutiques, you will discover an array of unique souvenirs, artwork, and Hawaiian treasures to bring back with you.*

# Local Markets and Shops

Maui is renowned for its diverse local markets and shops, showcasing a range of unique souvenirs, handmade crafts, fresh produce, and artisanal products. Here are some top spots to explore on the island:

### Maui Swap Meet:
Taking place every Saturday morning at the University of Hawaii Maui College campus in Kahului, this bustling market boasts a wide array of vendors offering handmade crafts, jewelry, clothing, artwork, and more. Visitors can discover special gifts and local treasures here.

### Lahaina Craft Fair:

Held weekly on Sundays at Lahaina Gateway shopping center, this fair features local artisans selling handmade jewelry, ceramics, paintings, and other distinctive creations. Live music and food vendors add to the lively atmosphere.

### Maui Ocean Center Store:

Found at the Maui Ocean Center in Ma'alaea, this store stocks marine-themed gifts, educational items, and souvenirs inspired by Hawaii's marine life. From apparel to books, visitors can find a variety of items relating to conservation efforts.

### Upcountry Farmers Market:

Situated in Kula, this market, held on Saturday mornings at Kulamalu Town Center, offers locally grown produce, artisanal food products, baked goods, and crafts, providing a taste of Maui's agricultural scene.

## Paia Town:
Known for its eclectic shops along Baldwin Avenue and Hana Highway, Paia offers surfwear, handmade jewelry, and art in its galleries and boutiques, ideal for unique finds.

## Makawao Town:
In Upcountry Maui, this charming town features historic architecture, art galleries, and boutique shops showcasing local artists' work, crafts, and treats, creating a quaint shopping experience.

## Whalers Village:
Located in Ka'anapali, this shopping complex houses a mix of boutiques, retailers, and souvenir shops offering clothing, jewelry, and Hawaiian gifts. A dining option with ocean views adds to the experience.

## Queen Ka'ahumanu Center:
Maui's largest shopping mall in Kahului provides a diverse range of stores, restaurants, and entertainment options, making it a one-stop destination for shopping, dining, and events.

These highlights the diversity and uniqueness of Maui's markets and shops, offering something special for every visitor, from handmade crafts to fresh produce and Hawaiian souvenirs.

## Souvenirs and Gifts

There is a wide variety of souvenirs and gifts to choose from in Maui that capture the essence of the island's culture and natural beauty. Here are some popular options to consider bringing back from your trip:

### Local Artwork:
Look for paintings, prints, and photographs by local artists that showcase Maui's landscapes, marine life, and cultural heritage. Art galleries and craft fairs are good places to find unique pieces.

## Hawaiian Jewelry:

Consider buying handmade jewelry made from materials like Koa wood, black coral, pearls, and seashells. Look for pieces with traditional Hawaiian designs.

## Hawaiian Quilts:

These feature intricate designs inspired by nature and cultural motifs. You can find beautifully crafted quilts in shops across Maui.

## Local Food and Treats:

Bring home Maui-made food products like coffee, macadamia nuts, honey, jams, and chocolates. You can also get fresh produce or tropical fruits.

## Hawaiian Apparel:

Shop for Hawaiian shirts, dresses, sarongs, and aloha wear made from colorful fabrics with traditional prints.

### Lei and Fresh Flowers:
Purchase a fragrant flower lei or a bouquet of fresh flowers to enjoy the beauty and aroma of Maui's flora.

### Handcrafted Souvenirs:
Look for wooden carvings, ceramic pottery, coconut shell products, and woven items like baskets as keepsakes of your time in Maui.

### Local Books and Music:
Explore Maui's cultural heritage through books and music celebrating Hawaiian history, legends, and traditions.

By choosing souvenirs that reflect Maui's beauty, heritage, and talent, you can bring home a piece of the island's aloha spirit to cherish and share with others. Whether it's artwork, jewelry, local food, or a lei, your souvenir from Maui will be a special reminder of your time in paradise.

# Chapter 10: Safety and Laws in Maui

Remain safe and well-informed during your visit to Maui! Familiarize yourself with local regulations, traffic rules, and safety guidelines to guarantee a pleasant island stay.

# Health and Safety Tips

When preparing for a trip to Maui, it is crucial to prioritize your health and safety for a positive and trouble-free experience. Here are some essential health and safety suggestions for Maui travelers:

### Stay Hydrated:
It is vital to drink plenty of water, particularly in Maui's warm and humid weather. Keep a reusable water bottle with you and make sure to refill it regularly, especially when participating in outdoor activities or being under the sun.

## Use Sun Protection:

Shield your skin from the sun by wearing sunscreen with a high SPF, UV-protective sunglasses, and a wide-brimmed hat. Reapply sunscreen every few hours, particularly after swimming or sweating.

## Practice Safe Swimming:

Exercise caution when swimming or snorkeling in Maui's ocean waters. Stick to lifeguarded beaches whenever possible, heed warning signs, and be attentive to beach conditions. Watch out for strong currents, rip currents, and dangerous surf conditions.

## Respect Marine Life:

Avoid touching or disturbing marine life, like sea turtles and coral reefs. Maintain a safe distance and observe marine animals from afar to minimize disruption to their natural habitat.

## Stay Informed About Weather Conditions:

Stay informed about weather predictions and potential risks, such as high surf or flash floods.

Regularly check local weather updates and adjust your plans accordingly, especially if engaging in outdoor activities.

**Be Mindful of Wildlife:**
Show consideration for Maui's wildlife by refraining from feeding or approaching wild animals. Keep a safe distance and observe wildlife respectfully to avoid disrupting their natural behaviors.

**Practice Responsible Tourism:**
Reduce your environmental impact and honor local customs by sticking to designated paths, properly disposing of waste, and supporting sustainable tourism practices and eco-friendly businesses.

**Seek Medical Aid if Necessary:**
If you encounter any health issues or emergencies during your time in Maui, seek medical help promptly. Familiarize yourself with nearby medical facilities, urgent care centers,

and hospitals, and ensure you have any required medications or medical supplies on hand.

By adhering to these health and safety guidelines, you can have a safe and enjoyable trip to Maui while ensuring your well-being and showing respect for the environment and local community.

## Emergency Contacts

When traveling to Maui, it's important to be aware of emergency contacts in case you need assistance. Here are some important emergency contacts for Maui:

### Police, Fire, and Medical Emergencies:
Dial **911** for immediate assistance in the event of a police, fire, or medical emergency. Emergency dispatchers will connect you to the appropriate authorities who can provide assistance.

## Maui Police Department (Non-Emergency):

If you need to report a non-emergency situation or request police assistance that is not life-threatening, you can contact the Maui Police Department's non-emergency line at **(808) 244-6400**.

## Maui Fire Department (Non-Emergency):

For non-emergency situations or inquiries related to fire safety or services, you can contact the Maui Fire Department's non-emergency line at **(808) 270-7561**.

## Emergency Medical Services (EMS):

If you require emergency medical assistance or an ambulance, dial **911**. EMS personnel are trained to provide medical care and transportation to hospitals or medical facilities in case of medical emergencies.

## Poison Control Center:

In case of accidental poisoning or exposure to toxic substances, you can contact the Hawaii

Poison Control Center at **1-800-222-1222** for immediate assistance and guidance.

## American Red Cross - Hawaii Chapter:
The American Red Cross provides disaster relief, emergency assistance, and support services to residents and visitors in Hawaii. You can contact the American Red Cross - Hawaii Chapter at **(808) 734-2101** for assistance or information.

## Coast Guard - Search and Rescue:
If you encounter a maritime emergency or require assistance at sea, you can contact the U.S. Coast Guard - Sector Honolulu for search and rescue operations at **(808) 842-2600**.

## Visitor Information and Assistance:
For general information, assistance, or inquiries related to tourism, attractions, accommodations, and activities in Maui, you can contact the Maui Visitors Bureau at **(808) 244-3530** or visit their website at www.visitmaui.com.

It's a good idea to program these emergency contacts into your phone or keep them readily accessible during your visit to Maui. In case of an emergency, stay calm, provide clear and accurate information to emergency responders, and follow their instructions for assistance and support.

# Local Laws and Regulations

To have a safe and enjoyable visit to Maui, it's crucial to be familiar with the local laws and regulations. Here are some important rules to keep in mind:

### Traffic Rules:
Follow traffic laws like driving on the right, obeying speed limits, and always wearing seat belts. Hawaii has strict laws against driving under the influence.

## Smoking Rules:
Smoking is not allowed in certain public areas, so use designated areas to avoid fines.

## Alcohol Laws:
The legal drinking age is 21, and it's illegal to drink in public places. Public intoxication can lead to fines or arrest.

## Littering:
Dispose of trash properly to maintain Maui's beauty and avoid fines.

## Marine Protection:
Respect marine laws to preserve Hawaii's marine ecosystems by following guidelines for activities like snorkeling or boating.

## Cultural Etiquette:
Show respect for Hawaiian culture by following local customs and traditions.

## Wildlife Safety:
Keep a safe distance from wildlife and avoid feeding or approaching them to protect the animals and avoid legal consequences.

## Permits and Regulations:
Obtain permits for activities like camping or hiking in protected areas, following guidelines to comply with environmental protections.

Following these laws and regulations not only ensures a responsible visit but also contributes to preserving Maui's natural beauty and respecting its cultural heritage. Consult local authorities for guidance or assistance regarding specific laws.

## Useful and basic Hawaiian Language

Learning some basic Hawaiian language phrases can enhance your experience and show respect for the local culture during your visit to Maui. Here are some useful and basic Hawaiian language phrases to know:

**Aloha:**
[ah-LOH-hah] - Hello, goodbye, love, affection, compassion; the most commonly known Hawaiian word, used as a greeting and farewell.

**Mahalo:**
[mah-HAH-loh] - Thank you; express gratitude and appreciation.

**A hui hou:**
[ah hoo-ee hoh-oo] - Until we meet again; a farewell phrase expressing the hope of seeing someone again.

**E komo mai:**
[eh KOH-moh my] - Welcome; an invitation or greeting extended to someone entering a place or joining a group.

**Ohana:**
[oh-HAH-nah] - Family; refers to one's immediate or extended family, as well as close friends and community members.

**Mahalo nui loa:**
[mah-HAH-loh NOO-ee LOH-ah] - Thank you very much; an expression of deep gratitude and appreciation.

**Keiki:**
[KAY-kee] - Child; used to refer to a young person or child.

**Makai:**
[mah-KAI] - Toward the sea; used to indicate direction toward the ocean or seaward.

**Mauka:**
[mow-KAH] - Toward the mountains; used to indicate direction toward the mountains or inland.

**Pau hana:**
[pow HAH-nah] - Finished work; after work; refers to the end of the workday or a social gathering after work.

**Kokua:**
[koh-KOO-ah] - Help, assistance; a request for aid or support, or an offer of assistance.

**Ono:**
[OH-noh] - Delicious, tasty; used to describe food that is enjoyable or satisfying.

**Wahine:**
[wah-HEE-neh] - Woman; used to refer to a female person or woman.

**Kane:**
[KAH-neh] - Man; used to refer to a male person or man.

**Hale:**
[HAH-leh] - House; dwelling; used to refer to a house, home, or building.

**Honu:**
[HOH-noo] - Sea turtle; a common Hawaiian word used to refer to sea turtles, which are revered in Hawaiian culture.

**Hana hou:**

[HAH-nah ] - One more time; encore; a request for a repeat performance or action.

**Pono:**

[POH-noh] - Righteous, just, moral, correct; refers to a sense of balance, harmony, and integrity.

Practice these basic Hawaiian language phrases and use them respectfully during your time in Maui. Embracing the local language can help you connect with the culture and community, fostering a deeper appreciation for the island's unique heritage and traditions.

# A 7 Day Itinerary in Maui

Here's a 7-day schedule for discovering the key attractions of Maui:

**Day 1: Lahaina Arrival and Relaxation:**
Arrive in Maui and settle into your lodging in Lahaina, a lively historic town.

Spend the afternoon exploring Front Street with its array of shops, galleries, and eateries.

Enjoy a waterfront dinner while witnessing the sunset over the Pacific.

**Day 2: Road Trip to Hana:**
Embark on the famous Road to Hana, a picturesque drive along Maui's rugged coast.

Stop at various viewpoints, waterfalls, and cultural sites like Ho'okipa Lookout, Twin Falls, and the Seven Sacred Pools.

Visit Hana town for its shops, beaches, and cultural sites.

Return to Lahaina for relaxation after a full day of exploration.

## Day 3: Molokini Crater Snorkeling:

Go on a boat tour to Molokini Crater, renowned for its clear waters and diverse marine life.

Enjoy snorkeling or scuba diving to see colorful fish, coral, and maybe turtles or manta rays.

Relax on the boat with lunch and refreshments before heading back to Lahaina.

## Day 4: Upcountry Maui and Haleakalā:

Drive to Upcountry Maui for its farms, views, and the Ali'i Kula Lavender Farm.

Visit the summit of Haleakalā for breathtaking island views.

Take a scenic hike or just admire the volcanic scenery in Haleakalā National Park.

Return to Lahaina for a farm-to-table dinner.

## Day 5: Beach Relaxation:

Unwind on one of Maui's stunning beaches like Ka'anapali Beach or Wailea Beach.

Engage in water activities or a beachside massage.

Witness the sunset and dine at a waterfront eatery nearby.

## Day 6: Iao Valley and North Shore Exploration:

Explore Iao Valley State Park and hike to the iconic Iao Needle.

Learn about Hawaiian culture at the park's visitor center.

Visit Paia and Makawao on Maui's North Shore for their shops, cafes, and galleries.

Enjoy local treats and browse boutiques before returning to Lahaina for dinner.

## Day 7: Departure:

Take a final walk along Front Street and grab any last-minute souvenirs.

Check out of your accommodation and head to the airport, reminiscing about your incredible Hawaiian vacation.

This itinerary features a blend of relaxation, adventure, and cultural discovery, allowing you to experience the best of Maui's natural beauty, outdoor activities, and local charm.

# Final Thought

As you get ready for your trip to Maui in 2024, there are some final thoughts and tips to remember to ensure an unforgettable and enjoyable experience on the Valley Isle.

Maui has a lot to offer for everyone, from its beautiful beaches and landscapes to its vibrant culture and thrilling outdoor activities. Whether you want to relax or seek adventure, Maui has it all.

Exploring Maui's natural beauty, like the iconic Road to Hana and Haleakalā's summit, should be a priority in your plans. Take the time to soak in the island's stunning landscapes.

Immersing yourself in Hawaiian culture is a must-do while in Maui. Attend a luau, discover the island's history at cultural sites, and enjoy authentic Hawaiian cuisine for a truly enriching experience.

Maui provides a variety of accommodation options to suit different preferences and budgets, ensuring a comfortable stay during your trip.

The culinary scene in Maui is diverse and delightful, offering a range of delicious dishes inspired by local ingredients and global flavors. Don't miss out on sampling fresh seafood and traditional Hawaiian specialties.

Renting a car gives you the freedom to explore the island at your own pace, while guided tours offer convenient ways to experience top attractions and activities.

It's essential to show respect for Maui's environment, community, and traditions. Practice responsible tourism, support local businesses, and leave no trace to help preserve the island for future generations.

Maui is a paradise with its natural beauty, cultural experiences, and exciting adventures awaiting you. Whether you seek relaxation, adventure, or cultural immersion, Maui will leave you with cherished memories and a desire to return to the magic of the Valley Isle.

Made in the USA
Las Vegas, NV
10 May 2024

89773399R00069